Andreas Gloge

I fell asleep reading and woke up dreaming

— Poems & Poesie —

Bibliografische Information der Deutschen Nationalbibliothek:
Die Deutsche Nationalbibliothek verzeichnet diese Publikation in
der Deutschen Nationalbibliografie; detaillierte bibliografische
Daten sind im Internet über https://dnb.dnb.de abrufbar.

Lektorat: Martina Gloge
Buchcover & Layout: Martina Gloge
www.martinagloge.com
Herstellung und Verlag:
BoD – Books on Demand, Norderstedt
ISBN: 978-3-744-81510-9

Wer aufmerksam sucht,
wird einiges finden ...

Vorwort

Wir alle starten am gleichen Punkt mit den gleichen Voraussetzungen: Eine Handvoll Buchstaben und dazu einige Satz- und Sonderzeichen.

Das ist alles. Mehr haben wir nicht. Mehr brauchen wir nicht.

Jedes Stück Weltliteratur, jeder Bestseller, jedes noch so schnell vergessene Gedicht ist aus einer überschaubaren Zahl an Zeichen und Symbolen entstanden. Je nach Sprache sind es ein paar mehr oder weniger.

Nun gilt es einfach nur, diese Zutaten stets aufs Neue in eine möglichst spannende Reihenfolge zu bringen. Ich hoffe, es ist mir hier gelungen.

Vielleicht verändern die Handvoll Buchstaben in diesem Buch etwas in dir und sorgen für ein besonderes Gefühl, womöglich sogar für Inspiration. Und wenn nicht, dann hast du wenigstens deinen englischen Wortschatz trainiert. Denn fast alle der folgenden Texte sind auf Englisch. So oder so: eine Win-win-Situation!

Ach ja, es geht im Folgenden übrigens um Träume und wilde Feenmagie, um die Kraft der Natur, um Licht und Dunkelheit und den bunten Nebel dazwischen.

Das alles folgt dem kleinen aber bedeutsamen Wunsch, einfach etwas zu erschaffen, das vorher nicht dagewesen ist. Ein simpler Gedanke. Ein unbestimmtes Gefühl. Etwas nicht Greifbares. Und das alles durch eine Handvoll dunkler Buchstaben und Zeichen auf hellem Papier.

Das ist alles. Mehr haben wir nicht. Mehr brauchen wir nicht.

allem
ANFANG wohnt
ein ZAUBER inne

PART I

INTO THE HEART OF GREEN

HOME

People tend to forget
that nature is home.

This is where
we come from.

This is where
we'll go.

And they tend to forget
about the pixie dust, too.

zur Nacht *hin*

Zur Nacht hin kehrt die Stille ein.
Dann klingen unsere Gedanken
am lautesten.

Und wir hören,
was wir träumen.

moving the
world

They stored the books in an old marble hallway
out of sight
our of mind
next to the worm eaten desk
with that dusty ancient globe on it
that got touched only
by the earliest golden sunbeams every morning.

Little did they know
what they had done
because the books eagerly
bathed in the golden morning's warmth
and thereby learned everything
about everything
the sun had ever seen:
all the tales of mankind and more.

And then the books whispered to each other.
Word by word.
Tale by tale.

And so whispers filled the vast void
of the old marble hallway
and on the worm eaten desk
the ancient globe
listened.

And the globe
understood.

And by that
simple words were able
to move the world.

"

And then the books *whispered* to each other. Word by word. Tale by tale.

"

spotting the

fairies

Sometimes it's easy to spot the fairies.

The trick is
        to blink with open eyes
    while silently humming
                to your own heartbeat
    while standing on one leg
                with both feet on the ground
        while taking a picture
            against the sun with your lens closed.

As I said:
    just a piece of cake,
            really...

...but don't get caught!

CLASH

of

clouds

Poseidon knew nothing of a climate crisis
but only that one day
the endless rain would come
and thereby from behind the heavenly veil
the sea would become the world
and all the madness of mankind
would be washed away
into oblivion
by a clash of clouds
(and all the living
good hearts and souls too)

the green *whispers*

The children had never heard
about the green whispers.
They followed the rustling of the leaves
and climbed up
and into the old tree
that has been waiting here for centuries
only never to be seen again.

Return

to **Wonderland**

One morning a mild breeze
coming right from the forest
joined the buzzing of bees
and HER wilderness' chorus.

HER world was burning
with leaves of jade
and emerald flowers
in an aquamarine shade.

The sea of joy
was HER meadow of carats;
I jumped and I drowned
like the drunken parrots.

She washed me bleak
She cleansed my soul
She ate my heart
With teeth of coal

That night I returned
to lay in YOUR bed;
my hair full of bees
all crushed and all dead.

So I washed you bleak
I cleansed your soul
I ate your heart
with teeth of coal

" "

She ate my heart. With *teeth* of coal.

" "

shooting

stars

That's beautiful,
they said ...

Those are shooting stars,
they smiled ...

... but they were simple folk
and never knew
anything about
the winged truth
between heaven and earth
and the endless hunger
of divinity.

the
little
ones

The Little Ones
vanished
from the sight of men and women
ages ago.

The old tongues spoke of them
in awe and fear.

Now the Little Ones sleep
down in the deep.

Waiting for the day to reclaim
their Emerald Throne and to reshape
the earth into everlasting
green.

spring is *coming*

made of ice and snow and pure blue crystals
the transparent creature awoke

just for the blink of an eye

as when its icy gaze froze
in fear
it realised

that in the moment
of its snowcold creation

sundawn
was about to caress the land

with dashes
of deathly
melting
warmth
and
light

pipe

dream

AVALON
lost in mist and time

forever
out of reach

but always
in my eye line

there is no

come on, you dreamer
 let yourself go
        to
          setting sails

        into the unknown

   crossing crystal blue oceans and endless skies
                       shooting with cannons
            full of stardust and fairybreath

      at cunningly dodging dreams that might
   (if you hit them)
          become the future

        when you wake up

EVERSILVER

MONOLITH

The EVERSILVER MONOLITH
once
was like Saturn-Cronus
— *all-devouring* —
feeding on everything breathing
and
any on mortal's days and hopes to come

until TIME
caught up with it

and it slowly started fading
into a broken and crumbling
God
left with nothing but its own myth
that flickered for eons and ages
and then finally faded into its well deserved
oblivion

we are

nature

Taking care
of nature generally speaking means
taking care
of our environment.

Meanwhile our environment is
taking care
of us
allowing us
to live
by nourishing us
with warmth, light, water, air and
a solid and fertile ground underneath our feet
and by giving us
eternal beauty.

So taking care
of nature generally speaking means
taking care
of ourselves.

Because
we are
nature.

let there be **light**

(and darkness)

There is light.

And there is darkness.

We reach out.
We try to make an impact.
We try to leave a mark.

But what we really do leave
behind is nothing but a shadow
on a wall that one day will be nothing
but dust
in the curious eyes of newborn stars.

Because we are light.
And we are darkness.

                                        And that's okay.

PART II

INTO THE MIND OF COSMICANDY

COSMICANDY

– The Haiku Series –

Exploring the multiverse with eternal appetite for silly space adventures and the sweet sensational thrills lurking in the shadows of puzzling wordplay and haikus.

EPISODE 1

goosebumps in the suit
a future with no tomorrow
good plans always change

EPISODE 2

only gravity
underneath the icy moon
defines ups and downs

EPISODE 3

I see what I am
a million broken shades but
complete from afar

EPISODE 4

a detective knows
the colours of emotions
inevitably

EPISODE 5

do not fear the fear
when elements shake the world
your strength lies within

EPISODE 6

easy to get stuck
pure sweet dreams of luring light
tasting fading dust

EPISODE 7

a cavern of thoughts
outsider on the inside
believe in rituals

EPISODE 8

looking for treasure
under the fading rainbow
always out of reach

EPISODE 9

everything is quiet
in the heart of frozen wilds
longing for some pulse

EPISODE 10

open the closed door
one meaningful step by step
silently cheering

EPISODE 11

back to earth and grass
nature's breath filling my lungs
longing to lay down

EPISODE 12

ready to take off
full of anticipation
no seatbelt needed

EPISODE 13

someone else's plan
biting on your cracking spine
get your blaster out

EPISODE 14

caught in the circle
playing the part is the deal
do not close your eyes

EPISODE 15

a wish is a wish
every magic has a price
don't trust the Genie

EPISODE 16

paralyzed in dreams
every move strains the muscles
no real strings attached

EPISODE 17

drowning in bubbles
laughing with soaking sadness
no end in plain sight

EPISODE 18

goodbye means hello
the calm silence of retreat
space sabbatical

PART III

INTO THE HERE AND NOW
(AND EVERYTHING ELSE)

a romance of **shadows**

two lonely spirits are waiting
for the train to bring them home

she could start the conversation asking
him about his dreams
he could ask her about
her life in a faraway past

but all they do is staring into
the night
when all the others are fast asleep
their visions enlightened by oblivious neon lights

a romance of two
shadows
melting into one

until the arrival of the electric dragon
takes the silent princess away
mixed with the first rays of a shy morning sun
her last look through the dusty window
proclaims the end of a silent affair
leaving the prince all by himself at the platform
with the hint of a bittersweet smile
around his lips

MOTHS

Sometimes a flickering candle
is more than just
some burning wick on wax
as that shining beacon for the lost
longing for warm fire
is the death call for the weak
blinded by their funeral pyre.

I am

your

killer

inside

You never cared to look at me.
You never cared to care.
You never touched my gaze
or knew my face.

And still you will remember me
like an old and vibrant melody;
and still you will
keep on humming me
deep inside your memory.

I was always at your side,
always willing to fight your fights.
I was there from dusk till dawn
like an old forgotten thorn.

I never dared to look at you.
I never dared to share.
I never touched your gaze
because you should never know my face.

For I am a killer
of many loves and hearts and dreams;
and though I do not want to mourn
I will kill more like a deadly poisoned thorn.

And only you will remember me
like an old and vibrant melody;
yes, only you will keep on humming me
deep inside your memory.

"

And still you will *remember me*
like an old and vibrant melody.

"

gambling

hearts

This feeling
makes the world
vibrate with vivid colours.

Love
is blindness.

Can't you see?

First Aid Poetry

for the **puzzled heart**

(gone down the gutter)

Your eyes shimmer like
anapestic amethysts making
my legs shiver every
iambic pentameter of the way.

And while your sighed syllables are
prophecies of trochaic wonders
born in ancient pyrrhic times
I soundlessly whisper into the catalexis
off
beats
to overcome the pervasive patterns which
open up your metrical door for every stranger
with a dactylic promise…

So give me a line-break
of
caesura,
pierce me with your pun;ct.u-at'ion of
headlessly ɹǝʌo sʅǝǝɥ verse
and please, please, please, no more of this
endlessly enigmatic incomplete syntax
like you are tiptoeing
on a twisted wire in a möbius-strip-circus.

Can't you see I am nothing but
an alliterative amorous adventurer and
really not longing for poetic enchantment anymore
in reason or rhyme –
so gimme a dime for every time I drink fine vine
to make me forget
about you –
as I am no longer looking
for sense because I lost
all my senses
in your amphibrachic web
of life lies and pipe dreams
full of howling vowels prowling foully
into my rotating spondaic heart.

Alas, no more stanza needed;
but if there has ever been
some kind of romance in chivalrous balladry
you sucked it all in with your Babel Fish weirdness
and torturing tenderness of illustrious illusions.

Long story short:
I really dig your diphthong, ay!

"

please, please, *please*, no more
of this endlessly enigmatic
incomplete syntax

"

HOW TO WRITE

BEST$ELLERS

After I wake up

I hiccup
  words

            I dreamt up

    to make up
stories

        that shake up

  my own
      expectations

Train of **thought**

seats full of strangers and voices and sounds

but everything fades away
except for my heartbeat and breath
when I see your eyes

through glass and mirror
looking back at me like promises

shimmering above the damp dark land outside

while the moonless morning
remembers our moonlit night before

and me wishing that the train conductor would
already be announcing the next stop:

tonight

another frozen

goodbye

outside our window
there awakes a world in bloom

the tender morning zephyr strokes the land
a blue sky above the ancient mountains
and melodious poems
filling the warm air from treetops

our bed is still warm
my skin still tingles
your laughter still rings in my ears

you are dreamily singing our old songs
while my eyes are betraying my frozen smile

outside our window
there awakes a world in bloom

why am I so damned afraid of melting?

Mantra
for the daily
rise & shine

Come on now!
Get up!
Get up on your knees

and life will give
you
pleasure and joy
with
snow in spring
and
birdsongs to sing.

Come here now!
And run!
Run as fast as you can

and don't forget
to breathe
as the life that you live
demands that you must
love equally your magic
and dust.

circle

of

life

terminus means end

end means death

death means beginning

beginning means change

change means expecting

expecting means acting

acting means proceeding

proceeding means finishing

finishing means terminus

band**lands**

(a silly britmix)

Soft razorlight beams
were kissing my eyelids
and I awoke from deep purple dreams
of beatles rolling on stones
and iron maidens celebrating black sabbath
in their placebo police homes.
Knowing that no muse could cure
my anathema blur of writer's bloc party
I rose up from my stony bed being sure
that a new order's clash in my editor's radiohead
could revive that queenlike oasis of artistic genesis
so I'd be a starsailing someone who creates instead.
Outside arctic monkeys were coldly playing
hot-blooded killers with snow patrol rifles
while hard-fi athletes were stereophonically swaying.
I threw back my suede head to lift
the turin brakes with manic street preaching vibes
that gave me the right art brut shift.
My veins that once mistook tears for fears
were now cleared of all kasabian white lies pulp
to open up my divine comedic weary ears.
Suddenly a keane verve filled my heart
with a depeche mode of sweet talk talk
and kooks' promising a brand new but heavy start.

Then the jamiroquaian smiths helped me call
friends like Travis, Jesus and Mary on the chain
or fratellis pinky Floyd and Franz Ferdinand and all.
And I waited for them at the mercy sisters' archive
where a led zeppelin was already rising
with Florence and her machine to finally drive
me, myself, my mind and soul
into futures of musical bliss
to feel alive and to feel whole.

"

Suddenly a keane verve filled
my heart with a depeche mode
of sweet *talk talk*

"

the wisdom of **people**

Inside the endlessly expanding void
of knowledge and limited human perception
it felt like there was nothing to hunt for anymore
and nothing to gain.

So the people decided to remain still
and in silence
in the corner of here and now
and they kept waiting

for the return of long gone hopes and dreams that
once escaped in those endless corridors
of their puzzled and selfish minds.

And so they waited for
nothing
until it was too late to change
anything
and so they returned to
nothing
inside the endlessly expanding void of
a universe
they did not understand or
cared about.

Stupid.

SpiEgelBilder

DER SEELE

Im Frühling meines Lebens
war der Sommer meine liebste Jahreszeit,
wegen der Art, wie die warmen Nächte rochen,
wenn ich mit Musik im Herzen durch die
schlafenden Straßen nach Hause lief.

Im Sommer meines Lebens
entwickelte ich eine Vorliebe für den Herbst,
denn er schenkte mir das goldene Laub
und das zwiegespaltene Verlangen nach
bittersüßpoetischer Vergänglichkeit.

Jetzt zu Beginn vom Herbst meines Lebens
umfängt der Frühling meine Gefühle
mit dem Gesang der Vögel zum Sonnenaufgang,
der Freude an aufkeimenden Blüten und Blättern,
und der Hoffnung auf ein zufriedenes Jahr.

Was erwartet mich wohl im Winter meines Lebens?
Vermutlich kristallklare Luft mit dem Zauber
der Gewissheit, dass alles Leben
nur Transformation ist und die Jahreszeiten
nur Spiegelbilder der Seele.

HEY!

(this day is **for you**)

Open the window.
  Take a deep breath.
    Feel the sun.
     The rain.
      The wind.
The cold and the warmth.

        Follow the rainbow.

        Stay calm.
        Be kind.

  Call a friend.
Write am message to a loved one.

    Think about life.
      Think about your life.
Think about nature.

  Make good art.
    Read a book or two.

        And never forget:

          This day
          is for YOU!

PART IV

THE END IS NOT THE END

Atme ein. Atme aus. Atme ein. Atme aus. Atme ein.
Atme aus. Atme ein. Atme aus. Atme ein. Atme aus.
Atme ein. Atme aus. Atme ein. Atme aus. Atme ein.
Atme aus. Atme ein. Atme aus. Atme ein. Atme aus.
Atme ein. Atme aus. Atme ein. Atme aus. Atme ein.
Atme aus. Atme ein. Atme aus. Atme ein. Atme aus.
Atme ein. Atme aus. Atme ein. Atme aus. Atme ein.
Atme aus. Atme ein. Atme aus. Atme ein. Atme aus.
Atme ein. Atme aus. Atme ein. Atme aus. Atme ein.
Atme aus. Atme ein. Atme aus. Atme ein. Atme aus.
Atme ein. Atme aus. Atme ein. Atme aus. Atme ein.
Atme aus. Atme ein. Atme aus. Atme ein. Atme aus.
Atme ein. Atme aus. Atme ein. Atme aus. Atme ein.
Atme aus. Atme ein. Atme aus. Atme ein. Atme aus.
Atme ein. Atme aus. Atme ein. Atme aus. Atme ein.
Atme aus. Atme ein. Atme aus. Atme ein. Atme aus.
Atme ein. Atme aus. Atme ein. Atme aus. Atme ein.
Atme aus. Atme ein. Atme aus. Atme ein. Atme aus.
Atme ein. Atme aus. Atme ein. Atme aus. Atme ein.
Atme aus. Atme ein. Atme aus. Atme ein. Atme aus.
Atme ein. Atme aus. Atme ein. Atme aus. Atme ein.
Atme aus. Atme ein. Atme aus. Atme ein. Atme aus.
Atme ein. Atme aus. Atme ein. Atme aus. Atme ein.
Atme aus. Atme ein. Atme aus. Atme ein. Atme aus.
Atme ein. Atme aus. Atme ein. Atme aus. Atme ein.
Atme aus. Atme ein. Atme aus. Atme ein. Atme aus.
Atme ein. Atme aus. Atme ein. Atme aus. Atme ein.
Atme ein. Atme aus. Atme ein. Atme aus. Atme ein.

Kiša pada,
trava raste.

(Der Regen fällt,
das Gras wächst.)

Nachwort

Ich hoffe, es hat dir gefallen und du bist vielleicht sogar ein wenig ins Träumen, Grübeln oder Schmunzeln geraten.

Möglicherweise hast du sogar Lust, irgendwann (in ferner oder naher Zukunft) nochmal durch die Seiten zu blättern – oder dieses kleine Büchlein an Freunde, Familie und Bekannte weiterzuempfehlen. Es würde mich freuen.

Und nicht vergessen: Gedichte bestehen nicht nur aus Buchstaben und Worten, sondern vor allem aus Gedanken und Gefühlen – und die verändern sich mit der Zeit und geraten zudem gern mal durcheinander. Und das ist okay.

Andreas

www.andreasgloge.com